Fruit

Edited by Rebecca Stefoff

Text © 1994 by Garrett Educational Corporation

First Published in the United States in 1994
by Garrett Educational Corporation,
130 East 13th Street, Ada, Oklahoma 74820.

First Published in 1991 by A & C Black Publishers Limited
with the title Fruit, © 1991 A & C Black Publishers Ltd.

Manufactured in the United States of America

Library of Congress Cataloging-in-Publication Data

Moss, Miriam.
    Fruit / Miriam Moss.
        p.   cm.—(Threads)
    Includes index.
    ISBN 1-56074-059-0
    1. Fruit—Juvenile literature.   2. Cookery (Fruit)—Juvenile
literature.   3. Fruit-culture—Juvenile literature.   [1. Fruit.]
I. Title.   II. Series.
TX397.M67   1994
641.3'4—dc20
                                                    94-19349
                                                        CIP
                                                        AC

Fruit

Miriam Moss

Photographs by Robert Pickett

Contents

GEC GARRETT EDUCATIONAL CORPORATION

All kinds of fruit

Fruit comes in all sorts of shapes, sizes, and colors.
How many fruits can you name on this page?
(Answers on page 25.)

Looking at fruit

Fruit is good for you because it contains carbohydrates, which give you energy, proteins, which help you to grow, and vitamins, which keep you healthy. But fruit is mostly made up of water.

Some fruits are hard and crunchy, some are soft and juicy. The prickly pear on the right feels rough and spiky, but the plum is smooth. Compare the textures and tastes of some other kinds of fruit.

Inside some fruit there are pips or stones. They are the seeds of the fruit. Guess how many pips are rattling inside an apple? Did you guess correctly? A mango has one big seed and so has an avocado. Sometimes we eat the seeds of fruit, but not if they are hard or big. A kiwi fruit is pitted with black seeds. Try and find the seeds in a satsuma and a banana.

Sometimes you have to peel off the skin to find the part of the fruit you can eat. Peel an orange. Can you smell the droplets of oil that squirt out of the holes in the skin? Which other fruits need peeling?

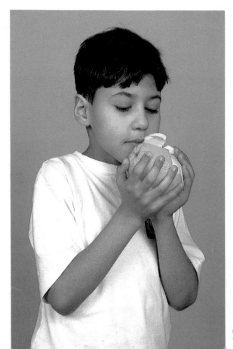

What is fruit?

Fruit grows on plants, bushes, or trees. The fruit is the fleshy part of the plant, protecting the seeds.

Apples grow on apple trees. In warm spring weather, green leaves appear on the tips of the branches. Then flower buds grow on the twigs. The buds open out into flowers, called blossom. Inside each flower there are tiny stalks, called stamens. The stamens are the male part of the flower. The tops of the stamens are covered with a yellow dust called pollen.

Bees and other insects visit the flowers to look for the sweet nectar inside them. Sometimes the pollen sticks to the insects' bodies. When an insect visits another flower, the pollen may rub off on to the stigma, which is the female part of the flower. If this happens, a tiny hard, green apple may begin to grow behind the petals of the flower. As the apple grows, the flower dries up and the petals fall off.

The apple is attached to the tree by a strong, bendy stalk. Food and water from the tree travels to the apple through the stalk. Hold up an apple by its stalk. Can you see the dried up parts of the flower underneath?

During the summer months, the sunshine helps the apple to grow bigger and sweeter. In the autumn, it is ripe and ready for picking. Then the leaves fall from the apple tree. During the cold winter months, the tree conserves its energy.

Travelling seeds

The seeds inside fruit can grow into new plants. To grow, each seed needs its own space, light, and food, so the seeds have to be carried away from the plant on which they grew.

Birds and animals eat brightly colored berries and fruit seeds. The seeds pass unharmed through their bodies. These seeds may take root in the soil and grow into new plants.

Some seeds are scattered by the wind. The sycamore seed has "wings" to help it travel a long way, and the burdock has hooks that catch on to passing animals or people's clothes. Find out about seeds that grow in pods.

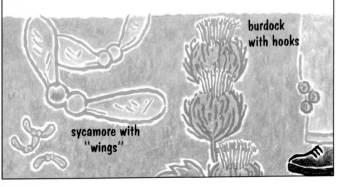

burdock with hooks

sycamore with "wings"

Fruit that falls from trees is called windfall fruit. The fruit rolls away from the tree and as the flesh rots, the seeds may sink into the soil and take root.

A nut is a fruit. It is a single seed inside a hard shell. Coconut seeds travel across oceans. The seed is protected from sea water by the shell. When the coconut is washed ashore, the milk inside provides enough food to start the seed growing into a coconut palm.

Fruit is an important food for wild animals. Squirrels eat fruit, such as the acorn, which is poisonous to humans. Can you think of any other fruits that animals eat?

Different kinds of fruit

Fruit can be sorted into different groups. Some fruits can belong to more than one group.

A berry has seeds covered by soft pulp or pith. Not all berries are small and round as you might expect. Some berries, such as citrus fruits, have thick skins. All the fruits in this picture are berries.

Bananas, pineapples, mangoes, star fruit, and papaws grow in tropical countries, where it is very hot and rainy. They are often called exotic fruits.

Apples and pears are hard fruits. Usually, they grow in cool or mild climates. In the autumn they are in season, which means that they are ready to eat.

Raspberries are soft fruits. Peaches, plums and cherries are stone fruits. Their hard seeds, or stones, are covered by soft flesh. Usually stone fruits grow in mild climates and are in season in the summer. In which month is your favorite fruit in season?

Make a collection of fruit and find out where each piece grew — you could look on the labels or ask your grocer. Draw a small picture of each of the fruits, showing what some look like when they have been peeled or cut in half. On a map of the world, pin the pictures to the place where the fruits grew. Don't waste the fruit you look at — you could use it to make a special fruit salad (see page 25).

Do the fruits in your collection come from the same places as the fruits on this map?

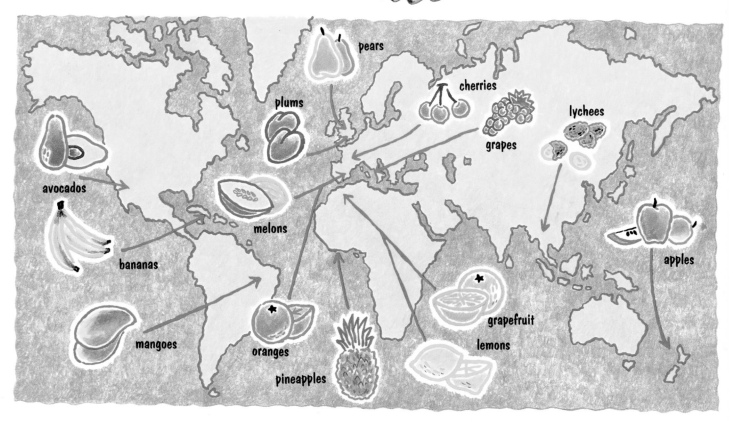

pears

plums

cherries

lychees

grapes

avocados

melons

apples

bananas

mangoes

grapefruit

oranges

lemons

pineapples

11

Fruit farming

Fruit trees and plants can grow in back gardens, in orchards, on hillsides, or on huge plantations.

In cool or mild countries, fruit growers plant orchards on the slopes of hills to stop frost and wind harming the fruit. They also try to make sure the trees grow in sunny places, where the fruit will ripen.

In this apple orchard, a man is pruning an apple tree before it bears fruit. He cuts back the branches so that more apples will grow and they will be easy to reach.

In hot countries, where it doesn't rain much, fruit trees need to be watered regularly. In this orange grove, a network of irrigation pipes carries water to the trees.

Many farmers protect their trees from fruit-eating insects by spraying the trees with chemicals called pesticides. The pesticides kill the insects. Always wash fruit before you eat it to make sure there is no pesticide left on the fruit.

Harvesting fruit

All over the world fruit is harvested when it is ripe and ready to eat.

Have you ever eaten a small, sour apple? It probably wasn't ripe. Sometimes you can tell if fruits are ripe without tasting them. Ripe melons and pineapples smell sweet. Fruits such as avocados, peaches, and mangoes are ripe when they feel soft. Gently press the top of an avocado. Is it ripe?

Some fruits look different when they are ripe. Which tomatoes in this bowl look ready to eat? What will make the unripe tomatoes change color? Find out what happens to a papaw as it ripens.

Ripe fruit that bruises easily is carefully picked by hand. Apple pickers pick only apples that are the correct color and size. They leave the other apples to ripen in the sun. Sometimes the apple pickers use ladders to reach the apples on high branches.

Strawberry pickers look under the leaves of rows of bushy strawberry plants for bright red strawberries. Some strawberry farms allow people to pick their own fruit.

Big bunches of bananas grow on tall plants which can be up to 18 feet high. Each bunch is made up of "fingers" of bananas, grouped into "hands" around the stem. Banana pickers climb the trees and cut down the green bananas. By the time the bananas reach the stores they will be ripe.

Not all fruit is picked by hand. Big machines are used to pick raspberries and cranberries.

Sorting and packing fruit

The freshly picked fruit is ready to be sorted and packed.

The apples are put in a trough of water and any dust or pesticide is gently washed away. Then the apples are lifted on to a conveyor belt and sorted according to size and color. Apples that don't look perfect are removed and dried or made into fruit juice. The first quality apples roll on to packing trays, which are stacked in a big box. Usually, there are one hundred apples in a box. When the boxes have been stamped with the name of the apple farmer and the date, they are ready to be taken to market.

How fruit gets to us

Most fruit has to be transported quickly so it is fresh when we buy it. Fruit from countries all over the world is sent to us by train, plane, boat, and truck.

Fruit that ripens quickly is transported in temperature-controlled containers. Try this experiment to find out why.

Put a ripe tomato into the refrigerator and put another ripe tomato on a window sill. Look at each of the tomatoes every day for a week. What happens?

Every day, crates of fresh fruit grown in the United States and in other countries are delivered to huge city fruit markets.

Early in the morning, when it is still dark, grocers and buyers for supermarkets arrive at these markets. They buy enough fresh fruit to sell in their stores that day. They take the fruit back to their market stall or stores where they arrange and price it, ready for customers to buy. Some fruits such as strawberries reach the stores only twelve hours after they were picked.

Preserving fruit

Some of the freshly picked fruit is stored and will be eaten later. This fruit must be preserved, otherwise bacteria will make it go bad.

Bacteria need water to live. Most of the water from dried fruit has been removed. Raisins are dried grapes. Leave some grapes and some raisins on a plate for a week. What happens?

Canned fruit has been heated to kill any bacteria, then sealed in airtight cans. Sugar is used to crystallize or preserve fruit in syrup. Pickling fruit in vinegar or freezing it are other ways of stopping bacteria from growing.

Guess how the fruits in this picture have been preserved.

Cooking with fruit

Chutney is a relish made from fruit, vinegar, spices, and sugar. Try making your own orange and lemon chutney.

You will need

1 large chopped onion

1 orange

1 lemon

a pinch of ginger powder

1-1/3 cups brown sugar

a pinch of salt

1/2 cup water

1/2 cup chopped raisins

1-1/2 cups malt vinegar

a pinch of cayenne pepper

a chopping board

a sharp knife

a wooden spoon

a large clean jam jar

a teaspoon

a large saucepan

a rubberband

a small circle of greaseproof paper to fit neck of jar

a large circle of greaseproof paper for lid

How to do it

1. Peel the orange and lemon and throw away the peel. Chop the fruit into small pieces. Put the chopped fruit and all the juice into the saucepan.

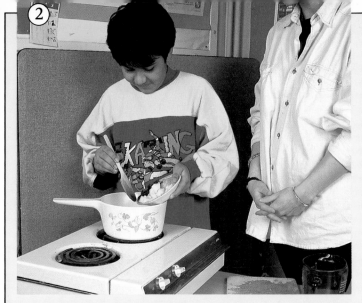

2. Add the raisins, sugar, ginger, and onion to the saucepan. Give the mixture a good stir and simmer on a low heat for about 5 minutes. Add the salt, cayenne pepper, water, and vinegar. Keep stirring the mixture until it is soft and thick. This takes about 15 minutes.

3. Ask an adult to help you pour the chutney into the jam jar.

4. Cover the top of the chutney with the small circle of greaseproof paper. Place the large circle of paper on top of the jam jar and secure it to the rim with a rubber band. Let the chutney cool. Spread it on sandwiches or serve it with rice.

Can you think of a nursery rhyme about citrus fruits?

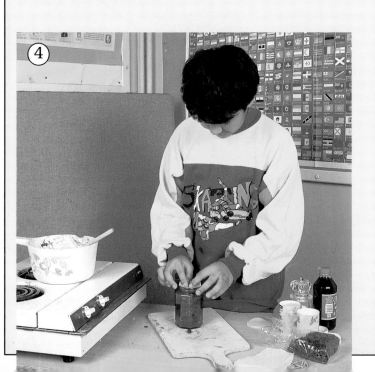

Fruit drinks

How many different kinds of fruit drink have you tasted? Look carefully at the labels on some fruit drinks to see if they are made with pure fruit juice. Some fruit-flavored drinks contain very little real fruit juice.

Try squeezing your own orange juice.

You will need

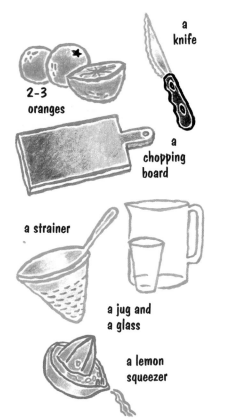

2-3 oranges

a knife

a chopping board

a strainer

a jug and a glass

a lemon squeezer

How to do it

Cut the oranges in half. Place half an orange on the squeezer. Gently push and twist the orange until no more juice will come out. Strain the juice into a jug. Find out how many oranges it takes to make a glass of fresh orange juice.

Some fruit juices can be fermented into alcoholic drinks. Wine is made from fermented grapes and cider from fermented apples.

Try making your own old fashioned lemonade.

You will need

3 lemons

a chopping board

1/2 cup brown sugar

a grater

a jug and a glass

a wooden spoon

a mixing bowl

a lemon squeezer

a strainer

3/4 quart boiling water (3 cups)

How to do it

1. Wash the lemons. Grate the rinds and place in the bowl. Ask an adult to help you pour boiling water over the rinds. Add the sugar and stir. Leave the mixture to cool.

2. Cut the lemons in half and squeeze out their juice. Add the juice to the liquid in the bowl.

3. Carefully strain the mixture into the jug. If your lemonade tastes too strong, dilute it with water. Keep the lemonade in the refrigerator.

23

A fruit fable

This story from Aesop's Fables is about a hungry fox and some grapes.

One day, a fox was trotting through a wood when he spotted a large, juicy bunch of grapes hanging high up on a vine. The fox was hungry and the grapes looked ripe and delicious. The fox tried jumping up to catch some of the grapes in his mouth. But however high he jumped the grapes were always just out of his reach. He became tired and angry as he jumped again and again. Soon the fox realized he would never reach the grapes. He walked away feeling disappointed. To make himself feel better, he muttered that the grapes looked small and unripe and would have tasted sour.

This is where the saying "sour grapes" comes from.

More things to do

1. Try making a special fruit salad. You will need a large pineapple and a selection of other fruit. Cut off the pineapple plume and keep for decoration. Scoop out the flesh from the rest of the pineapple and chop into small pieces. Keep the pineapple shell. Chop or slice the other peeled fruits. Mix up all the fruit with the juice of half a lemon and a tablespoon of sugar. Pour the fruit into the pineapple shell and serve with the plume on top.

2. Guess which fruits will sink and which will float in a basin of cold water. Did you guess correctly?

3. Cut various fruits in half and into different shapes. Dry the fruit on absorbent paper. Dip the shapes into paint and print fruit patterns on paper.

4. Apple bobbing is a good party game. Put some apples in a big bowl of water. Keep your arms behind your back and try to pick up the apples using only your teeth.

5. Make a fruity picture by illustrating the alphabet with fruit. Start with "A for Apple."

6. Find out about the story of Johnny Appleseed, the golden apple of discord which started the Trojan wars, and how Sir Isaac Newton discovered the laws of gravity.

7. Find out about the ancient custom of wassailing. Can you think of any other celebrations about fruit?

8. Weigh some mixed dried fruit, then soak it overnight in a bowl of water. Drain away the excess water and weigh the fruit again. What has happened?

9. Try growing fruit from seeds. Soak some melon seeds in water and leave in a warm place for 2 days. Plant the seeds in a pot of wet compost. Cover the pot with a plastic bag to keep in the moisture. It will be several weeks before the seeds start to grow.

10. Find out which of the following are fruits and which are vegetables: eggplants, rhubarb, peas, and runner beans.

1 banana 2 plum, orange 3 miniature pineapple, mango 4 pear, prickly pear 5 ogen melon, papaw 6 avocado, pomellon 7 apples 8 grapes 9 pineapple 10 star fruit, taradillo 11 strawberries 12 tangerines 13 pink grapefruit 14 raspberries & bilberries 15 lemon, lime, lychees 16 cherries 17 pomegranate 18 dates

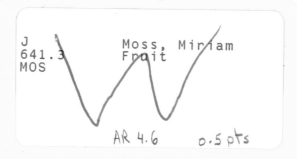